Such a joy – combining forms and colors.

I love bringing nature inside.

ith each treasure, a world of memories.

D1171116

A Gift for

Jamie
··

From

TROY
··
AIKMAN

Christmas, 2005

The Wonder of Birds

A Collection of Charming Discoveries

By Marjolein Bastin

Written and illustrated by Marjolein Bastin

Edited by Cynthia Musick

Art Direction by Steve Hess and Anne Simmons

© 2001, Marjolein Bastin

Manufactured for and © Hallmark Cards, Inc.

Kansas City, MO 64141

Printed in China

Assembled in China

ISBN 0-87529-869-9

How I envy the birds! They just flap their wings and off they go — while I must start a car or wait for a bus. And I would give anything to sing as they do — to express my feelings so clearly instead of searching for the right words.

I hope, after reading this book, you will never look at birds in the same way! You will slowly become "family" with them and see how much you are alike. When you see a familiar bird, you'll see him in a different way — noticing details, colors, and behavior that you've never noticed before. It is the same bird — the only one who has changed is you!

Come with me...I want to take you outside to join me for a walk! There's so much to discover!

Marjolein Bastin

PS: And this is only the beginning....

My Feathered Friends

Indigo Bunting

European Blue Titmouse

Meadowlark

Black-Capped Chickadee

Cardinal

Blue Jay

American Goldfinch

House Finch

Bluebirds

Winter Wren

Robins

Indigo Bunting

Sunflowers – we enjoy their golden faces... birds enjoy their tasty seeds.

I was overwhelmed when I discovered my first indigo bunting. He was picking ripe grass seeds in a field of yellow sunflowers.

I had to look two times before I could believe my eyes. What a powerful combination: the deepest shiny blue against that warm, full yellow of the sunflower petals!

Farther on, the female was feeding her baby. They were more difficult to see, since they both lacked the intense blue of the male. But muted brown is a much safer color when you are a clumsy teenager or a mother on a nest.

When you look at the indigo buntings' strong beaks, you realize that they are mainly seed eaters. I often see them feeding on thistles and goldenrods in the land between the river and my house. With endless patience, they nibble on grasses heavy with seeds. They seem especially fond of foxtail grass.

I don't know if it has to do with his splendid costume, but the male thinks it's enough to be a beautiful father-at-a-distance…he just sings a little here and there and shows off his beauty. Obviously, it works for them…I guess everybody has a different balance in a marriage.

So here is his wife in her dull dress, happily building the nest, laying the eggs — usually three or four — and hatching them patiently for 12 or 13 days. When at last the eggs hatch, it is often only the female that feeds the children.

A friend once gave me a beautiful indigo bunting nest that wasn't in use anymore. It is one of my treasures. It's the finest, tiniest nest I have ever seen, made of tightly woven grass, little roots, plant fiber, hair, and...all around it, neatly woven onto the base of the nest...a snakeskin. Can you imagine the bunting lady flying with that long skin in her beak? She has exquisite taste: snakeskin and the most chic husband in the world! MB

A nest like this is one of nature's miracles.

European Blue Titmouse

How could I leave out our European blue titmouse bird? He appears in so many of my drawings, and many of you will know him by now. He is the star of my favorite birdhouse lamp… he plays his role on many of my cards…it is obvious that I love him.

With his soft yellow colors combined with tender blue, black, and white, he is one of the most colorful birds of the Netherlands. Households there with nest boxes may have the slightly bigger coal titmouse in them or the blue titmouse. When you prefer the blue titmouse, just choose the box with the smaller opening.

Finishing touches make a house a home.

So many bird-watchers and bird-lovers started their hobby by watching the blue titmouse's family life. How exciting it is for a child to see this miracle...after a period of 18 days of feeding activities, the young birds leave the nest box — carefully, one by one — with a lot of vocal help from their parents.

For weeks, you see the baby blue tits around, busy and noisy — first clumsy, later more and more handy in hanging upside down from a fragile branch to catch that caterpillar, a nice mouthful of aphids, or a tasty spider!

Splish! Splash! Taking a bath!

C an you believe that while they grew up in that nest box, their parents fed them with more than 15,000 caterpillars? It is no wonder that farmers love to have these birds in their orchards.

Most baby birds start life on an insect diet. So why not hang a few nest boxes around your yard and throw away the bug spray! MB

They enjoy a "caterpillar lunch" in the beautiful trees.

Meadowlark

There is no need to explain where the meadowlark lives. He does indeed like meadows, pastures, and open fields as his name implies. It is there that he feeds, builds his nest, and raises his young.

With his brown-streaked back toward you, the meadowlark is difficult to see. Even when you discover him, your first thought might be that you see a quail...until he turns around and you see his proud breast, yellow as butter, as egg yolk, no, as sunshine!! There is not a yellow more intense — not even in my watercolor tubes. In addition, they wear as a necklace a big black "V" on their breasts.

In northern Missouri, the meadowlarks migrate to the south during the winter. So when I hear for the first time their flutelike whistle, "see-you-see-year", it means that spring has arrived!

YELLOW

I once saw a meadowlark on a pole in Kansas, and it amazed me that his song sounded completely different. I didn't understand it. I know now that there is an eastern and a western meadowlark. They are nearly the same, and the easiest way to tell them apart is by their song. That of the western is more melodious.

From my studio window, I look down at the fields and prairie around my house and can watch the meadowlarks chase after grasshoppers, locusts, and other grassland insects.

I never disturb birds near their nests. They are so vulnerable during that time — they might be so shocked by your presence that they never return to the nest, or your footsteps may guide a predator to the nest.

But a meadowlark makes her nest nearly impossible to find: she builds it under overhanging grasses, with a side entrance, not to be seen from the air (a good defense against overflying crows!). For extra protection, instead of flying directly to the nest, she lands at some distance from it and sneaks invisibly toward it through the grasses. Meadowlarks can be nesting right in front of me, but I have no idea where!

The female meadowlark lays white eggs dotted with light brown, especially on the bottom end. While she patiently sits on the eggs for 14 days, her husband keeps cheerfully singing and singing. I guess that is where we get the expression "happy as a lark"! MB

It won't be long before the meadowlark welcomes a new family.

Black-capped Chickadee

Among the first things I bought when I made an extended trip to America were a bird book and binoculars. I felt as if I possessed the golden key to nature's treasure box!

On my next walk through the rolling hills of Missouri, there was one bird I couldn't identify for a long time. It seemed that he was following me everywhere...through the woods, toward the river, from all directions: "pee-wee" — the "wee" lower in tone than the "pee" — and far away the answer, "pee-wee."

I grew more and more curious and even a little bit irritated, because I couldn't find the source of this conversation. I spotted chickadees similar-looking to the ones we have in Holland, but since their song is significantly different, I didn't think these were the "pee-wee" birds.

pee-wee, pee-wee

S oon I started answering "pee-wee" just to amuse myself so I wouldn't feel impatient. Finally, I read in the bird book that the black-capped chickadee has a song that is a whistled "pee-wee" — the first note higher.

I felt silly. How peculiar that the Dutch chickadee and the American chickadee look the same but have a distinctly different language — just like English and Dutch! When they are agitated, you can hear them communicate: "chicka-dee-dee-dee-dee!"

The chickadees enjoy their meal — what a wonderful sight!

Chickadees move around like little acrobats…and seem to see every movement. A chickadee is at my feeder all the time now. He loves the suet and sunflower seeds, which he takes one by one from the feeder to hammer in two on a nearby branch. The beaks of the chickadees are very small and fine, perfect instruments to pick the smallest insects from under bark or leaves.

When spring arrives, the chickadee will go back to the woods near the river, where he and his girlfriend will find a big old tree with a hole in the trunk to make their nest. Old trees are treasures for chickadees as well as owls, woodpeckers, nuthatches, and many other birds. Rotten wood is not that bad in nature!

But who knows? Perhaps the chickadees will choose one of my nest boxes for a home… because I am the Dutch lady who sings "pee-wee" so nicely to them!

MB

Cardinal

I'll never forget when I spotted my very first cardinal! I was on a nature walk on a rainy November afternoon in Missouri. The prairie landscape was so beautiful that day – painted in beige and gray colors. When I reached the bottomland near a small river, I suddenly glimpsed a powerful flash of incredible RED...my first cardinal! I could hardly believe my eyes! Immediately, I felt that this scene was meant to be a painting...a painting I started as soon as we were back in Holland.

Now the cardinal is an old, familiar friend. Since I spend part of my year in the United States, this fantastic bird has become my regular guest. I know his preference for sunflower seeds. I know that the female looks less spectacular with her warm beige breast, but she has the most beautiful lipstick-red beak, and both have big crests on top of their heads which can look very funny when the wind comes from behind.

When I hear a cardinal singing in a tree, I simply have to stand still. His song is so tender and sentimental, with loud, slow whistles. So touching that I wish I were a female cardinal.

The male cardinal's urge to feed his so-much-loved fiancée is often so great that he can't resist, even when they both are feeding from my well-stocked bird feeder. While she is busy eating, he interrupts her constantly with another tasty mouthful of sunflower seeds. She can hardly manage the amount and the speed. Perhaps this is his way of offering her a huge diamond engagement ring.

This reminds me of my "pre-engagement" time with Gaston, my husband. He often brought me tiny surprises of the kind he knew I would like: fossils, for instance, and shells, beautiful stones, feathers. It was one of the things that made me realize that we belonged together. And I saw the same thing happen with those two cardinals at my feeder.

SKIES

Marjolein Bastin

The cardinal's loosely built nest is mainly made by the female in four to nine days. I often find their nests safely in the middle of big prairie rosebushes. Clever... they are protected by hundreds of thorns.

Before she starts laying her eggs, they often take a sort of resting period, a honeymoon, of around five days. Then she lays three to four eggs. After they raise the first nest, there will follow a second and even a third. How nice that the tender, sentimental songs will continue for a long time to come! MB

Little cardinals have big appetites!

Blue Jay

Before I ever saw a blue jay, I knew him by his voice. I was in New York's Central Park, and I was so surprised to see all the birds there. I ran back to my hotel to grab my binoculars from my suitcase. On the way, I heard a very loud shrieking noise coming from somewhere among the leaves of a huge tree. What a voice! It certainly didn't sound shy to me!

I chose a bench and waited. Soon, out they came...two very, very beautiful blue birds gliding noisily down to enjoy a sip of water from one of the many fountains along the path. In a bird book I purchased the same day, I learned that this character was the blue jay. That was 13 years ago... my first short trip to the United States.

Just seeing the bluejay's feather, I can almost hear him.

The blue jay is my friend now, a regular visitor at my bird feeders in the United States. Brutal and self-confident, he chases away the hungry little birds and starts eating as if he were in a hurry to catch the train. Sometimes he takes peanuts with him to eat elsewhere in a quiet corner, or he buries them somewhere for a rainy day.

In the spring, his main foods are large insects, mice, eggs, young birds, or whatever other things may appear on his dining table. Even though it is difficult for us to think of the blue jay preying on our nature friends, he has to feed his family. Somewhere high in the trees, there is a nice nest of small branches where hungry young blue jays are begging for more and more and more...

In the fall and winter, his diet changes to acorns, beechnuts, and other fruits. Sometimes the jay hides his acorns, covers them loosely with a little soil, and nonchalantly decorates the place with some leaves or grass so that no one else can find them. Often the jay can't find them either, and something wonderful happens as a result. Many nice oak trees begin to grow in unexpected places, and without even knowing it, the clever blue jay slowly but surely builds his own territory with beautiful trees to nest in and many, many acorns to enjoy!

MB

Once a hidden acorn...now an oak tree for nesting.

American Goldfinch

On one of my first summer trips to America, I discovered a new, very colorful bird. Because I saw him first in the middle of the Midwestern prairie, I immediately named him "prairie canary." As soon as I bought my first bird book, I knew it was the American goldfinch.

The first time I saw him, he was in a field of bluestem grasses, black-eyed Susans, prairie coneflowers, and purple coneflowers. He landed on a big grass stem and slowly bent down into the colors of the flowers. I could hardly wait to start painting!

Now that I have had a chance to observe the goldfinches at my own bird feeders on the prairie, I have learned more about them. I know about their preference for the fine thistle seed that you can buy in every bird shop or supermarket. I know now that they don't disappear in the winter but simply molt their bright yellow feathers for a duller color. (After all, why should you wear that eye-catching color when you don't have to show off to find a nice girl?)

I also am familiar with the goldfinches' song now. I don't know exactly why, but I always feel so happy when I listen to them...as if life is happy and uncomplicated. "Per-chick-o-ree," says the bird book, and that's how it sounds, but I always am amazed by their personal interpretation.

I found a goldfinch nest last winter, and since it was not in use anymore, I could carefully inspect it. The inside was a neat, sturdy cup, tightly woven from thistledown and cattail down. I realized once more what great builders birds are... My fingers felt big and clumsy suddenly. I couldn't have made it.

A used goldfinch nest is also easily identified by a thick border of baby droppings around the nest rim. Most parents remove the droppings of their babies after each feeding and deposit them a distance from the nest. Goldfinches, however, don't care. Bohemians...

Since I know the strong relationship between thistles and dandelions and our friends the goldfinches, I have fewer problems with these weeds. No weed killer at my place! MB

Made with so much love...so delicate, so complete.

House Finch

For most of my life, I have lived in the country surrounded by nature's beauty. There was one time, however, when I did live in an apartment for a few months in the center of a busy city. Because I had never lived in a city before, it was exciting to experience something new…traffic day and night along the road, police sirens as an evening lullaby or a morning alarm clock, heavy trains making the ground tremble. Yes, it was new and exciting, but, oh…I missed nature so!

The ones who helped me through this time were the house finches! Between the busy road and my apartment was a narrow piece of no-man's-land which sloped downward. The tops of the trees growing there reached the window by my worktable. And that was the house finches' territory. When I listened to their voices singing their numerous songs and quarreling about territories, wives, husbands, and nesting materials, I could forget the city noises below.

Bringing a touch of country to the city…

Because they liked to live in cozy groups, I didn't have one pair to watch, but several. Every day, I enjoyed them more and more. Their antics always gave me something interesting to observe. Building a nest was more than a serious duty to keep the generations going — it was something fun! With passion, they flew back and forth with little sticks, grasses, beaks full of rootlets, plastic or paper, threads...you name it, and they could use it.

Their nesting possibilities were endless...a fork in the tree would be a good place, but so would a nest box, a hole in a tree, or the ledge on my apartment building. No problem for this bird!

In good company...what better way to spend an afternoon.

Originally, house finches lived only in the western part of the United States. These "Hollywood finches" were imported to New York as cage birds because of their beauty and their nice song. But because this wasn't allowed officially, sometimes the finches ended up being set free from their cages so their owners wouldn't get caught. Happy breeders that they are, they did what they had to do, and now we can enjoy them everywhere, east and west.

As you can see from the shape of their strong beaks, they mainly are seed eaters. When you want to spoil them, fill your bird feeders with sunflower seeds, and you will get a lot of joy in return!   MB

I love trading seeds for songs.

Bluebirds

When I discovered my first bluebird in the mountains of Colorado, I immediately thought of my paint box: What color should I pick to catch such a beauty? I found in my bird book that this was the mountain bluebird.

That was 10 years ago. Since then I have seen many bluebirds, not only the mountain bluebird, but also eastern and western bluebirds. I never get used to this heavenly color of blue and will always see it as though it were my first time.

When I glimpse a bluebird flying by, I see a gem, blue on gold, flashing in the sunlight. Once I saw several bluebirds in a field in late summer, grasses dry and golden in the warm afternoon sun. They were perching on a pole, overseeing every movement of the insects, diving now and then to the ground to catch them, blue on gold. Paradise can have no greater treasures.

So when a bird this beautiful is declining in numbers, there is immediate concern. Who wants to lose a bird of such beauty? Their decline came about because the house sparrow and starling, introduced to America from Europe in the mid-nineteenth century, wanted to nest in the same tree cavities and nest boxes as the bluebirds.

Luckily, the bluebird's beauty helped save him. People were concerned about losing this bird who brings happiness. Programs were started with long "trails" of nest boxes bordering fields — so that there were plenty of houses for sparrows, starlings, and bluebirds. Nest boxes were placed on poles to protect the birds from raccoons and snakes. And it worked!!! After years of declining, the number of bluebirds went up slowly.

Mother bird gives tender loving care... as well as a tender, luscious worm!

Recently, I hung a nest box close to my window, hoping a family of birds would make their home there so that I could observe them up close. I thought only an "ordinary" bird would be brave enough to nest so near me.

Soon, my joy couldn't be greater...I didn't dare to believe it when I discovered that bluebirds had moved in! Now I could follow them every day for weeks — even months, because they were there still in November, checking the nest.

When spring is in the air, I see them fall in love. He sings and waves one or two wings for her when they both sit on the railing of my deck. He shows her his favorite nesting place (yes, my nest box!), and she obviously likes it there. He follows her everywhere and brings her little snacks — a nice caterpillar, perhaps — to put her in the right mood.

Now they are not afraid of me anymore when I sit right next to them at my worktable. I love them, I admire them, and yes, they bring happiness!

MB

For the bluebirds - home...   ...for me - inspiration.

MB

Winter Wren

Birds attract me in so many delightful ways...their song may melt my heart...their color or behavior may catch my eye. Or I may even recognize myself in a bird. That is what happened to me with the winter wren.

Since my earliest childhood, this bird has always been nearby, building his nest in a box at our house or in the ivy which covered the walls. I recognized myself in that little brown bird — so small and difficult to spot, he seemed to be part of the background. I was always a shy girl and wanted to be like him — in the background.

But, ah, when that tiny bird starts to sing!!! You can't believe that this powerful song is coming from that tiny body — what volume! And not shy at all anymore, he perches on a spot where everyone can hear him, his whole body moves, his head turns, and he puts his whole heart in his song. Pure passion! As for me…my drawings are my songs!

The male winter wren uses his song to attract the female. He builds several nests, and when a female comes by, he tries to interest her in one of them by singing like crazy! She carefully inspects the nests, and if she loves one of these homes and its builder, she shows him her feelings by lining her favorite nest with feathers, wool, and down. I have even discovered pieces of insulation from our house in these winter wren dwellings!

So often I see myself in the busy little wren.

Much more common in America is the house wren. Difficult to tell them apart, other than by their size: the house wren is one inch bigger than the winter wren. Both wrens have tails that stick straight up in the air.

Now as I am writing this, it is spring. The wisteria around my studio in Holland is in full bloom. The scent of the flowers is around me. Right outside the door hangs the old nest box with the thatched roof. And I'm happy to see that the female winter wren is lining it again. Every year, these birds keep me company so pleasantly, and that is how it should be. In a few short weeks, a new generation of winter wrens will hatch...six eager mouths to feed... six new singers. MB

A flutter of housewarming gifts...

Robins

When I look back through all the drawings I have created in the past 20 years, I find that the European robin appears in many of them. He mainly shows up in my winter drawings when it is gloomy outside and we all need cheering up. And who can do that better than this bird with his warm orange-red breast and his big dark eyes. When all the other birds are silent in the winter, he still sings his sweet song...a song that sounds so tender, so varied that it melts your heart.

Among all the birds, the European robin seems the least afraid of people. When I work in the garden and turn the earth while weeding or dig a hole for a new plant, he looks from a distance, perhaps waiting for a nice earthworm. Often he perches on the shovel to have a better look. Once my daughter stretched out her arm toward him, and he flew to her and perched on her finger!!!

The children of the European robin look totally different from their parents. Where are their red breasts? Will they ever appear? There is a reason for being spotted, dotted, and brown when you are young: you blend into the background and are not as easily spotted by a crow or cat! That is helpful, since young birds just out of the nest behave very clumsily and are very noisy because they are hungry. They don't know how to catch their own spiders, worms, or moths. Eventually, the parents bring their young less and less food, so they finally understand they have to solve their hunger problems themselves.

Such a tasty snack... for such hungry children!

It reminds me so clearly of the time when my two children left home. The same sorts of things happened. It was so tempting to interfere, but I knew that in time, they would be capable of solving their own problems...just like the little robins, who do finally get their orange-red breasts!

Centuries ago, when the first settlers arrived in America, the cheerful American robin was given its name. For these newcomers, a new future was waiting. It was an exciting, insecure time, and many of the settlers were homesick. Even the birds were different in America. When they saw that bird with its warm red breast — a little like their robin, but a bit different — they knew what to name him: American robin! He made them feel at home, even if he was twice as big as the robin they knew from England.

I didn't know that history when we visited America those first years. I learned to love the bird that sang his pretty song from the trees which surrounded our hotel. "Cheerlee-cheer-up, cheerlee-cheer-up." I remember that he started singing as early as five in the morning, triggered by the bright streetlights of the city. I often lay awake then, nervous about the coming day but comforted by the strong voice of Mother Nature.

The robin often greets me with his wonderfully clear song.

Now we live in the country. I know that city robins start singing earlier than country robins. They nest now on a ledge outside my window. When building their nests, they gather material like people hunting garage sales. They use anything — grasses, plant stems, little roots or branches, plastic, paper — molded together with mud the female brings in her beak. For days they work, very concentrated — more the female than the male...but he accompanies her all the time.

Finally, everything is ready for the big event: she lays her four robin's egg-blue eggs — each day, one. And when she finishes, she sits there for nearly two weeks, patiently waiting for her eggs to hatch. When they do, we see both parents "worm hunting" on the lawn surrounding our house. The American robin often raises three complete families — and luckily, that just gives us more of them to enjoy! MB

I just love to watch the birds! And by using my binoculars, I can almost feel part of the bird families. Now that you've read about my discoveries, I'd like you to make some of your own. Across from this page is an envelope for you to add your own treasures. These can serve as reminders of the incredible discoveries and surprises that are around us every day in nature.

A single feather may recall the strikingly brilliant red of a cardinal; a photo of a robin may trigger memories of his wonderfully clear song; some twigs may remind you of the magnificent abandoned nest you'd discovered. Often the simplest things mean the most.

Bird watching can fill your days with a sense of wonder and the excitement of discovery. There's just so much to discover — more than enough for a lifetime!

Marjolein Bastin